OCTO®

Nemesis

Hard and Very Hard OCTO Puzzles

Tom,
HAPPY PUZZLING!
Doug Gardner

Doug Gardner

20 AUG 2016

Other OCTO® Books:

OCTO Unleashed
> 60 Octo puzzles ranging from Easy to Very Hard

OCTO Reloaded
> 60 Octo puzzles ranging from Easy to Very Hard

OCTO Genesis
> 60 Octo puzzles, only Easy and Medium

ISBN: 978-1-449-53570-4

Greetings!

In July of 2007, I set out to create a puzzle that would combine the basic concepts of Sudoku and Kakuro. After a few fits and starts, I came up with the construct you see on the following pages. This book is the fourth in a series of Octo books, aimed at puzzle lovers ready to face the full fury of the Octo puzzle.

I hope you enjoy them half as much as I've enjoyed creating and testing them...

Doug Gardner

Loving thanks to Alison, Madeline, and Isabel for their continued enthusiasm in support of the Octo Dream.

Special thanks to the Gardners and McBrides.

Many thanks to the testers, especially Jay, Pops, Matt, John M., Will B., Ethan, Carolyn O., Bill K. and family, Jimmy, Chip, Bill M. and family, David G. and family, Morgan, Kay, Brian M., Alicia, Paul, and the rest of my family at Trinity Presbyterian Church.

Very special thanks to Dennis, the hardest of the hardcore Octo puzzle testers.

Thanks to the early adopters: Greg, Pops, Will B., Sean, Ann, Ed S., Bill P., Kay, Ethan, David G. and family, Amy, random people on airplanes and in airports, and those university newspaper staffs willing to try something new.

OCTO® PUZZLES: INTRODUCTION, TIPS, AND TECHNIQUES

Introduction

Octo puzzles are unique because they require a wide variety of techniques to solve. If you have worked with Sudoku puzzles, you will be able to use most of the same general positional techniques that you use to solve Sudoku puzzles. If you are a Kakuro solver, the basic addition and factoring techniques will also be useful for solving Octos. The real fun and challenge for solving Octo puzzles is combining several techniques (and sometimes inventing new ones) to place numbers uniquely into the Octo grid.

First, let me introduce an Octo puzzle and some terminology:

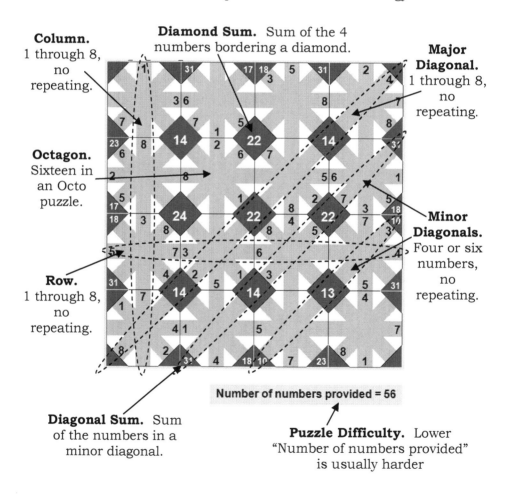

Column. 1 through 8, no repeating.

Diamond Sum. Sum of the 4 numbers bordering a diamond.

Major Diagonal. 1 through 8, no repeating.

Octagon. Sixteen in an Octo puzzle.

Minor Diagonals. Four or six numbers, no repeating.

Row. 1 through 8, no repeating.

Number of numbers provided = 56

Diagonal Sum. Sum of the numbers in a minor diagonal.

Puzzle Difficulty. Lower "Number of numbers provided" is usually harder

What's the Goal?

The goal of an Octo puzzle is to place the numbers 1 to 8 in each of the octagons such that the numbers are not repeated in any octagon, row, column, or diagonal. Major diagonals use each of the numbers 1 through 8. Minor diagonals use either four or six of the numbers 1 through 8 with no repeats.

The sums of the numbers in each minor diagonal are provided at the beginning and end of each minor diagonal. The sums of the four numbers that border each diamond are provided in each diamond. (The numbers that border diamonds do not have to be unique.)

This is all you need to know to get started, beginning with OCTO # 1 in the OCTO PUZZLES Section. For additional tips and strategies, read on.

Tips

Use a pencil. For all but the simplest Octos, you will need to note where numbers can and cannot correctly be placed. Eventually, as you continue to narrow down possibilities, you will need to erase and update your notations. Make sure you have plenty of eraser left on your pencil!

Use a variety of techniques. Start by filling in what you can using positional logic (the intersections of rows, columns, major diagonals, and octagons). Then use the Diamond sums and Diagonal sums to finish the puzzle. Diagonal sums become much more important as the puzzles get harder.

Be thorough. Especially for Very Hard Octos, you may have to methodically check each clue (row, column, diagonal, diagonal sum, and diamond sum) to collect enough information to solve the puzzle.

All of the puzzles in this book have been tested and are solvable with the clues provided.

Basic Solving Techniques

Your first strategy upon starting an Octo is to look for numbers you can fill in quickly.

1) Look for a row, column or major diagonal where most of the numbers are already filled in.

This number must be a **1** or a **3** because **2**, **4**, **5**, **6**, **7**, and **8** are already used in the column. Since **1** is already used in the same octagon, it must be a **3**.

Now you can fill in this number (**1**) because it's the only un-used number in the column.

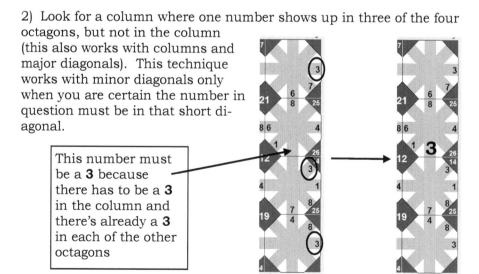

Keep in mind this doesn't work with minor diagonals, since they don't include all 8 numbers.

2) Look for a column where one number shows up in three of the four octagons, but not in the column (this also works with columns and major diagonals). This technique works with minor diagonals only when you are certain the number in question must be in that short diagonal.

This number must be a **3** because there has to be a **3** in the column and there's already a **3** in each of the other octagons

3) Three out of four numbers bordering a diamond sum will automatically give you the fourth number (in this case, **2** + **8** + **5** + **6** = **21**).

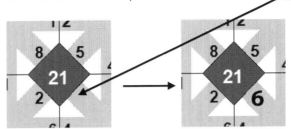

4) Often, having two of the four numbers around a diamond can be just as useful. In this case, you should test each number, **1** through **8,** and its "partner" to reduce the possibilities. In the following example, the numbers that go in the two circles have to add up to **11** (so all four numbers will add up to the diamond sum, **17**):

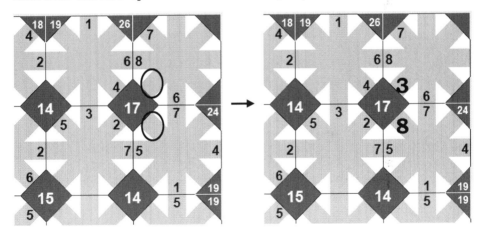

- The top circled number cannot be a **1** or a **2** because then the bottom number would have to be greater than **8** (**9** or **10**, respectively).
- The top number cannot be a **5** because there is already a **5** in the same diagonal.
- The top number cannot be a **6**, **7**, or **8** because those numbers already exist in the same octagon.
- That leaves a **3** or a **4** for the top number. However, if the top number is a **4**, the bottom number would have to be a **7**—but it can't be because there is already a **7** in the same octagon.

So, the top number must be a **3** and the bottom number must be an **8**.

5) Look for an octagon where one number is already in all but one row, column, and diagonal (I call this technique "Triangulation").

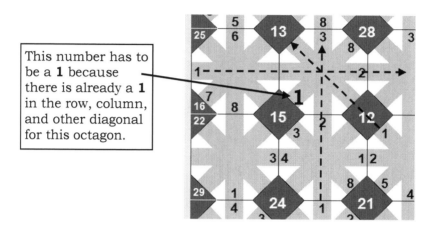

This number has to be a **1** because there is already a **1** in the row, column, and other diagonal for this octagon.

Advanced Solving Techniques

1) **Diagonal Factoring**. Minor diagonals and their diagonal sums are treasure troves of clues and are especially important for harder Octos. Your goal when working with minor diagonals is to figure which four or six numbers make up a minor diagonal by eliminating possibilities using the clues you have been given.

The simplest technique for eliminating number possibilities is to look for diagonal sums that only occur with one or two possible combinations of numbers. The following table illustrates:

Minor Diagonal (Four Numbers):

10	**1,2,3,4**
11	**1,2,3,5**
12	**1,2,3,6 or 1,2,4,5**
24	**3,6,7,8 or 4,5,7,8**
25	**4,6,7,8**
26	**5,6,7,8**

<u>Minor Diagonal (Six Numbers)</u>:

21	1,2,3,4,5,6
22	1,2,3,4,5,7
23	1,2,3,4,5,8 or 1,2,3,4,6,7
24	1,2,3,5,6,7 or 1,2,3,4,6,8
30	2,3,4,6,7,8 or 1,3,5,6,7,8
31	2,3,5,6,7,8 or 1,4,5,6,7,8
32	2,4,5,6,7,8
33	3,4,5,6,7,8

For example, if the diagonal sum for a four-number diagonal is **10**, you can eliminate **5**, **6**, **7**, and **8** as possibilities for all four of the positions in that diagonal.

Limited combination diagonal sums are also useful for identifying which numbers <u>must</u> be in that diagonal (the opposite of eliminating numbers). For example, if the diagonal sum for a six-number diagonal is **30**, you know that diagonal must include the numbers **3**, **6**, **7**, and **8** (although you won't necessarily know whether the other two numbers are **2** and **4** or **1** and **5** without more information).

2) **Working with Diagonals**. It is often possible to figure out that a particular number must be one of two along a diagonal inside a specific octagon. For example:

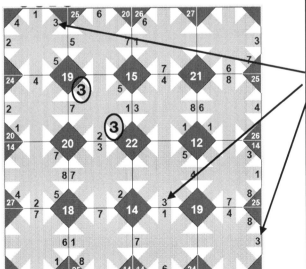

Since there are 3's in each of the other octagons along the major diagonal, the 3 for this octagon must be in one of the two circled positions.

I use the convention of writing the two choices in but circling both numbers so I know that this is an either/or situation (as shown here).

These "either/or choices" are very helpful, particularly for eliminating numbers within a given octagon or when diagonal factoring.

Now look at the six-number diagonal with the diagonal sum of **27**. There are four six-number combinations that sum to **27**:

2,3,4,5,6,7
1,3,4,5,6,8
1,2,4,5,7,8
1,2,3,6,7,8

However, none of the open positions in the diagonal can be a **1** because there are already **1**'s in each of the associated octagons (see the squared positions in the figure.) The only six-number combination that doesn't have a **1** in it is:

2,3,4,5,6,7

Of the combination **2,3,4,5,6,7**, the **4**, **5**, and **7** already appear in the diagonal, leaving the numbers **2**, **3**, and **6**. The open position in the middle octagon of the diagonal must be a **6** for two reasons:

- The numbers **2** and **3** already appear in that octagon (the **3** is due to the "either/or" determination made earlier), and
- There is already a **6** in the top octagon of the diagonal.

That leaves **2** and **3** for the top octagon in the diagonal. Although you can't determine which number goes in which position, knowing that two (and only two) numbers must be in two positions eliminates those numbers from being in any other positions in that octagon.

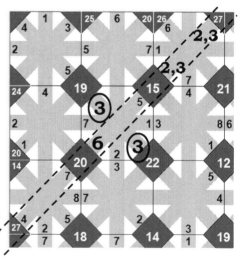

3) **Combining Techniques**. Look at the combination of the diagonal sum (**29**) and the diamond sum (**22**) . The possible six-number combinations that add up to **29** are:

2,3,4,5,7,8
1,3,4,6,7,8
1,2,5,6,7,8

The diagonal includes a **2**, **4**, and **8** which only matches the first choice:

2,**3**,**4**,**5**,**7**,**8**

That means the circled position must be either a **3**, **5**, or **7** (except it can't be a **7**, because there is already a **7** in the same octagon).

Looking at the diamond sum of **22**, the sum of the squared position and the circled position must be **10** (**22 - 4 - 8 = 10**). That means the squared position can only be a **7** or a **5**. However, the squared position cannot be a **7** because there is already a **7** in the same octagon—it must be a **5**. Remember that numbers adding up to a diamond sum are allowed to repeat, so **4 + 8 + 5 + 5 = 22** is okay.

We can now write in what we know about the rest of the diagonal. The only values left for the diagonal, (**3** and **7**), must go in the two open positions, although we don't know which of the two positions contains which number. Either way the **3** and **7** are placed, the triangle position must be a **7** (**20 - 3 - 7 - 3**).

Also, in the lower left octagon, the number **1** has to be in the hexagon position because there is already a **1** in the row passing through that octagon, leaving the last open position in the octagon for the number **3**.

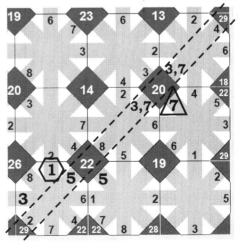

These are not all of the techniques you can use to solve Octo puzzles—just enough to get you started. I have found that the real fun of solving an Octo puzzle is using a variety of techniques in fun, challenging, and creative ways and in the process inventing your own solving techniques.

Enjoy, and Happy Puzzling!

Number of Numbers = 54 (Hard)

Number of Numbers = 54 (Hard)

Number of Numbers = 54 (Hard)

OCTO®

4

Number of Numbers = 54 (Hard)

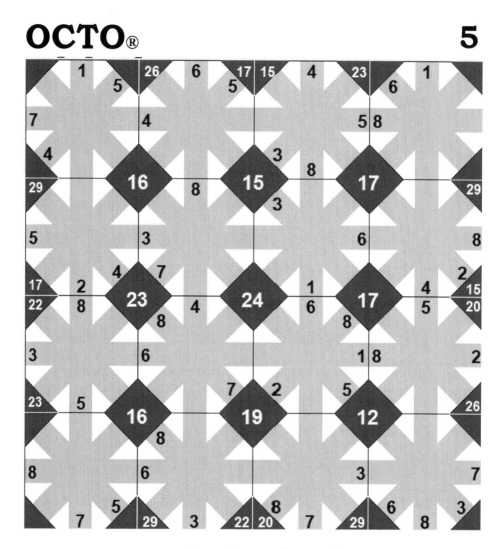

Number of Numbers = 54 (Hard)

OCTO®   6

Number of Numbers = 54 (Hard)

Number of Numbers = 53 (Hard)

Number of Numbers = 53 (Hard)

OCTO®

9

Number of Numbers = 53 (Hard)

Number of Numbers = 53 (Hard)

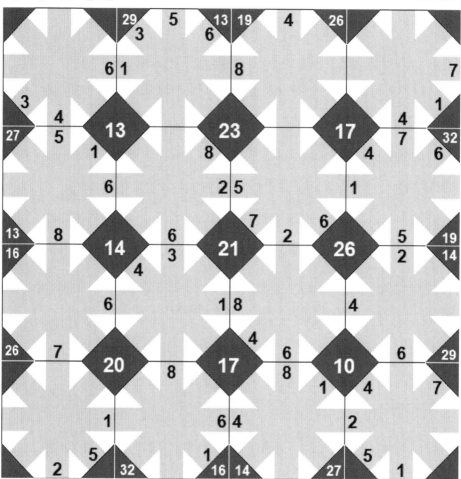

Number of Numbers = 53 (Hard)

Number of Numbers = 53 (Hard)

Number of Numbers = 53 (Hard)

Number of Numbers = 52 (Easy)

Number of Numbers = 52 (Hard)

Number of Numbers = 52 (Hard)

OCTO®

17

Number of Numbers = 52 (Hard)

Number of Numbers = 52 (Hard)

Number of Numbers = 52 (Hard)

Number of Numbers = 52 (Hard)

Number of Numbers = 51 (Hard)

OCTO® 22

Number of Numbers = 51 (Hard)

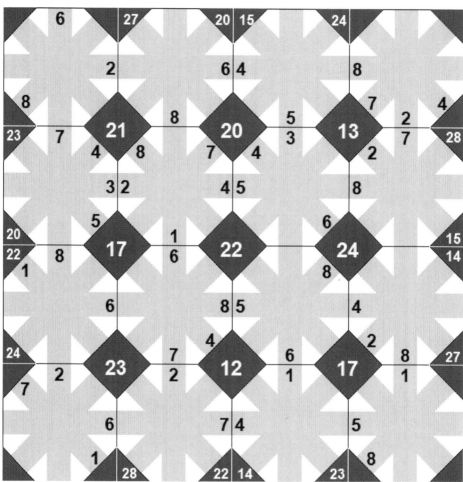

Number of Numbers = 51 (Hard)

Number of Numbers = 51 (Hard)

Number of Numbers = 51 (Hard)

Number of Numbers = 51 (Hard)

Number of Numbers = 51 (Hard)

OCTO®

Number of Numbers = 50 (Hard)

Number of Numbers = 50 (Hard)

OCTO®

Number of Numbers = 50 (Hard)

Number of Numbers = 50 (Hard)

Number of Numbers = 50 (Hard)

Number of Numbers = 50 (Hard)

Number of Numbers = 50 (Hard)

Number of Numbers = 49 (Very Hard)

OCTO®

Number of Numbers = 49 (Very Hard)

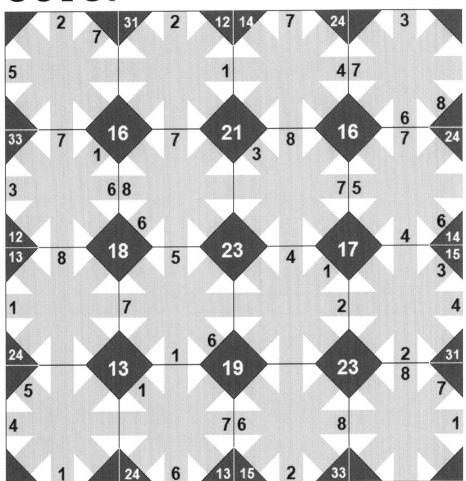

Number of Numbers = 49 (Very Hard)

Number of Numbers = 49 (Very Hard)

Number of Numbers = 49 (Very Hard)

OCTO®

40

Number of Numbers = 49 (Very Hard)

OCTO®

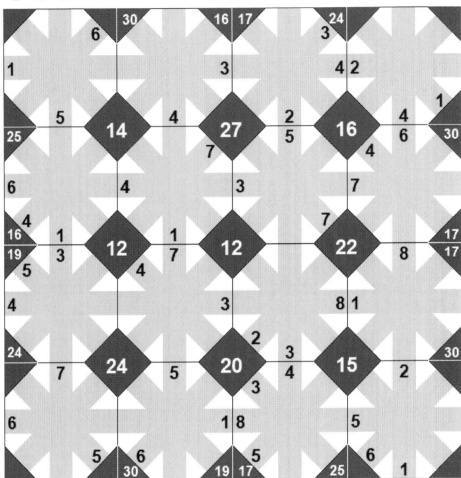

Number of Numbers = 48 (Very Hard)

OCTO® 42

Number of Numbers = 48 (Very Hard)

2	27		19	13		22		
5	6	7		4		8		3
7			2		3		4	6
29	6	**20**		**13**	5	**25**	7	29
	7			2		4		
	8	4				7		5
19			5			3		13
18	5	**21**		**19**	1	**24**		26
8				1		7		
6		8		3		4		1
22			4	2			3	27
	8	**14**		**16**	2	**21**	6	
								4
5		6				3		2
	3	29	1	18	26	29		
				6				

Number of Numbers = 48 (Very Hard)

OCTO®

Number of Numbers = 48 (Very Hard)

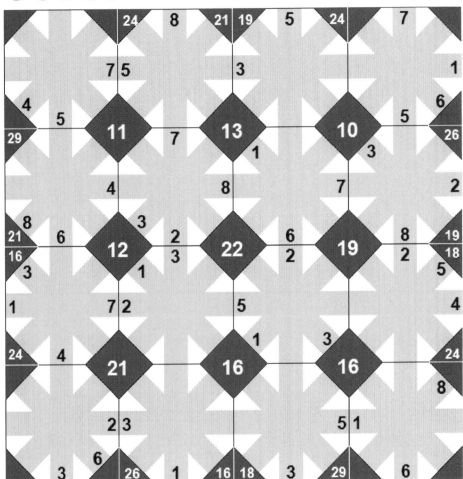

Number of Numbers = 48 (Very Hard)

Number of Numbers = 48 (Very Hard)

Number of Numbers = 48 (Very Hard)

OCTO® 48

Number of Numbers = 48 (Very Hard)

Number of Numbers = 48 (Very Hard)

OCTO® 50

Number of Numbers = 47 (Very Hard)

Number of Numbers = 47 (Very Hard)

OCTO®

```
    3        29   8    12 18   7    31        7
      5
4                    1            6 2
                              2              1
28    6    19    6    23        13          29
        1              8
4          1         5           8
        8                     4         5   18
12  5    20         14        20    4      22
22                            2
  3        3         7       7           5
5                    7           6 8
31  4    26    2    22        19          29
  6                                    6
4                  6 1                      5
  2                                1
    7    29   7    22 22   8    28
```

Number of Numbers = 47 (Very Hard)

Number of Numbers = 47 (Very Hard)

OCTO®

54

Number of Numbers = 47 (Very Hard)

Number of Numbers = 47 (Very Hard)

OCTO® 56

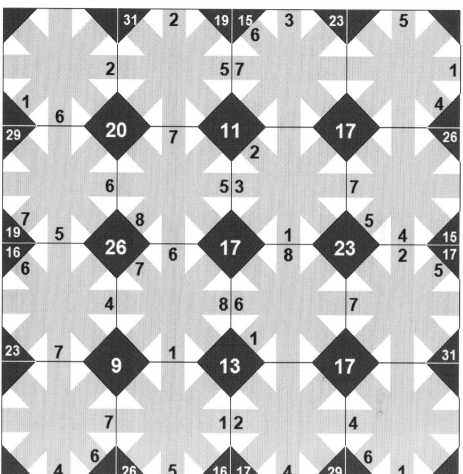

Number of Numbers = 46 (Very Hard)

Number of Numbers = 46 (Very Hard)

Number of Numbers = 46 (Very Hard)

Number of Numbers = 46 (Very Hard)

OCTO® 60

Number of Numbers = 46 (Very Hard)

SOLUTIONS

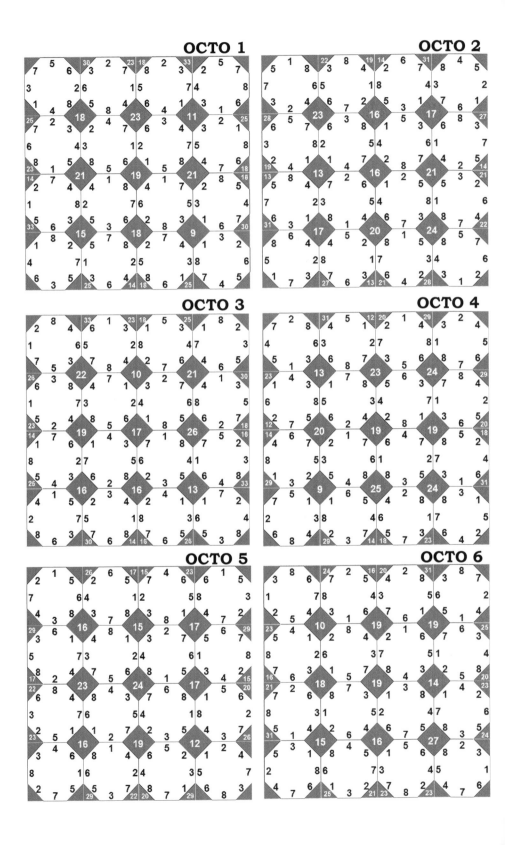

OCTO 7

OCTO 8

OCTO 9

OCTO 10

OCTO 11

OCTO 12

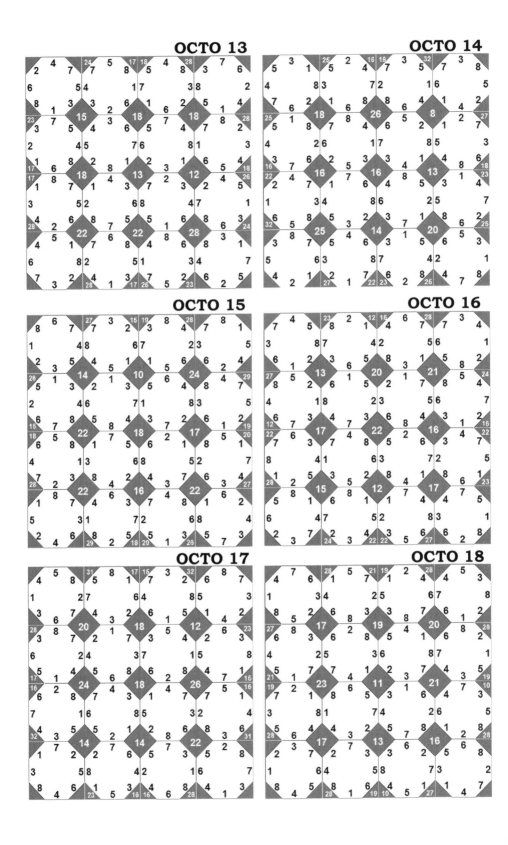

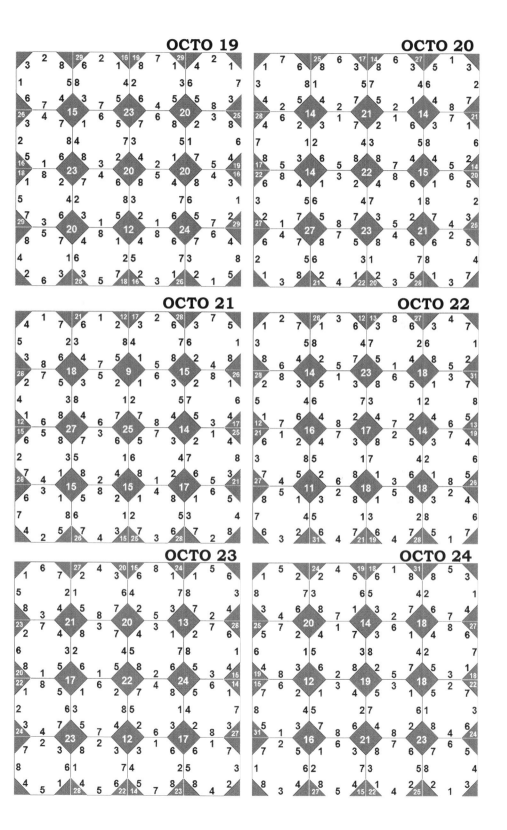

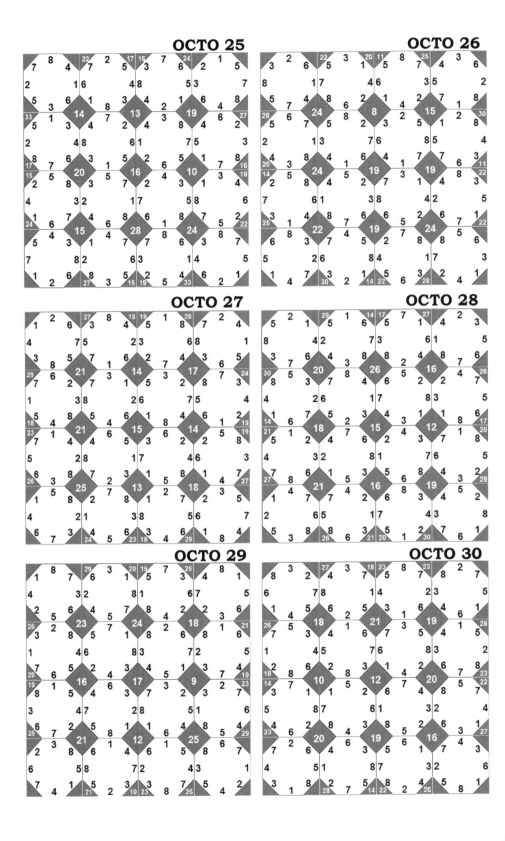

OCTO 25

OCTO 26

OCTO 27

OCTO 28

OCTO 29

OCTO 30

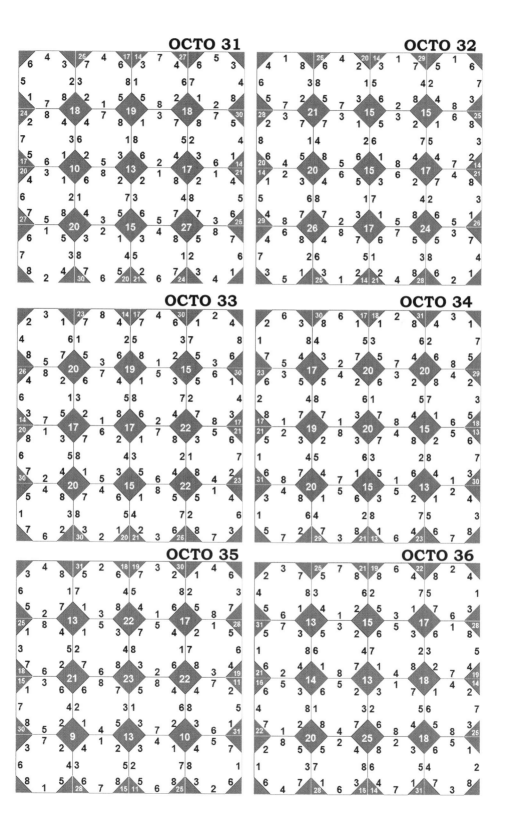

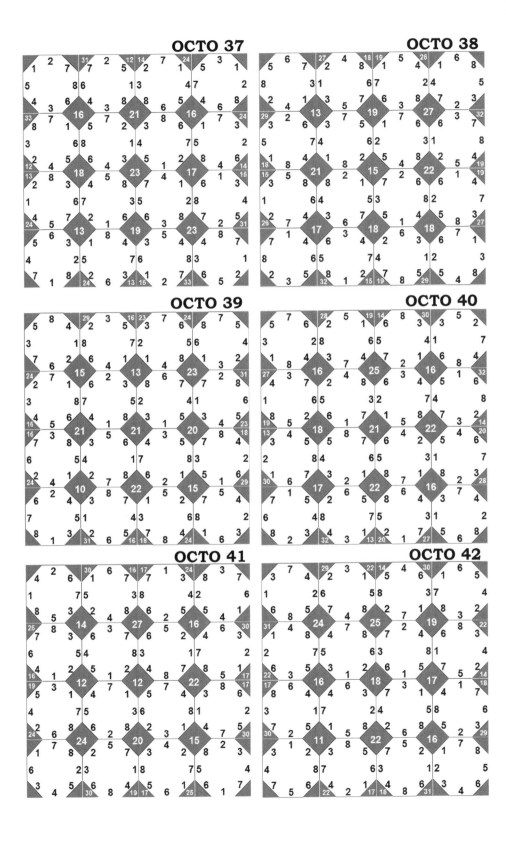

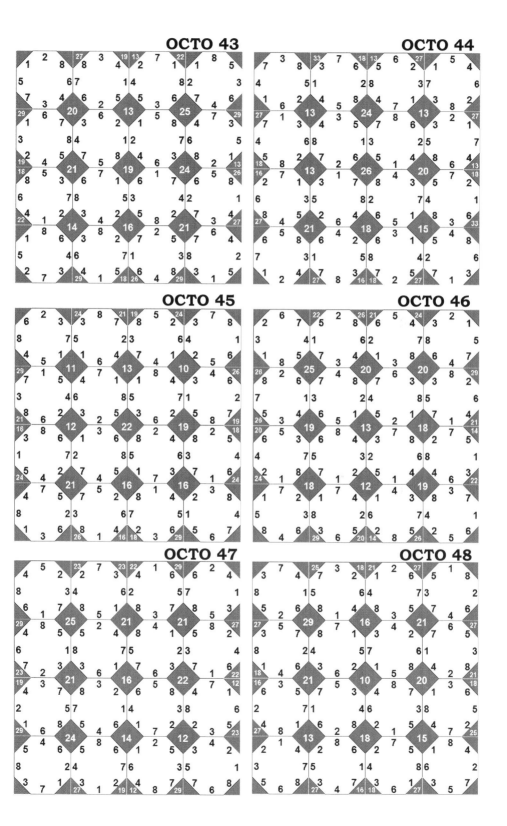

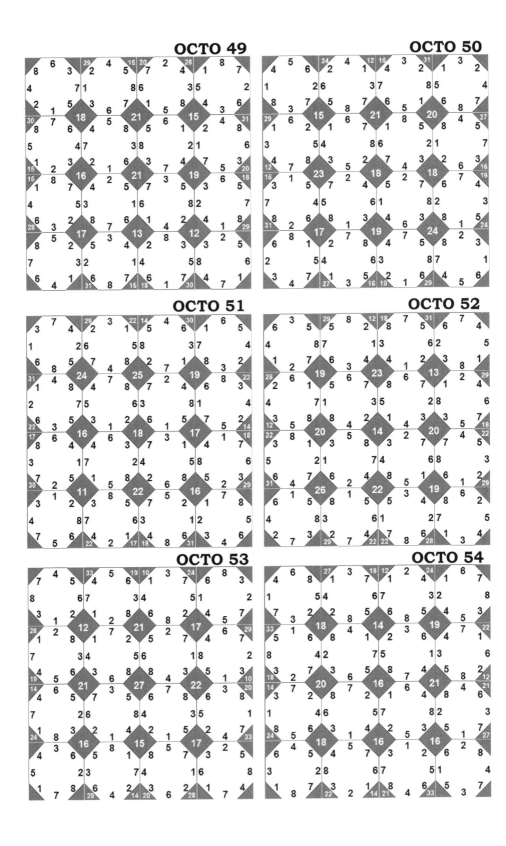

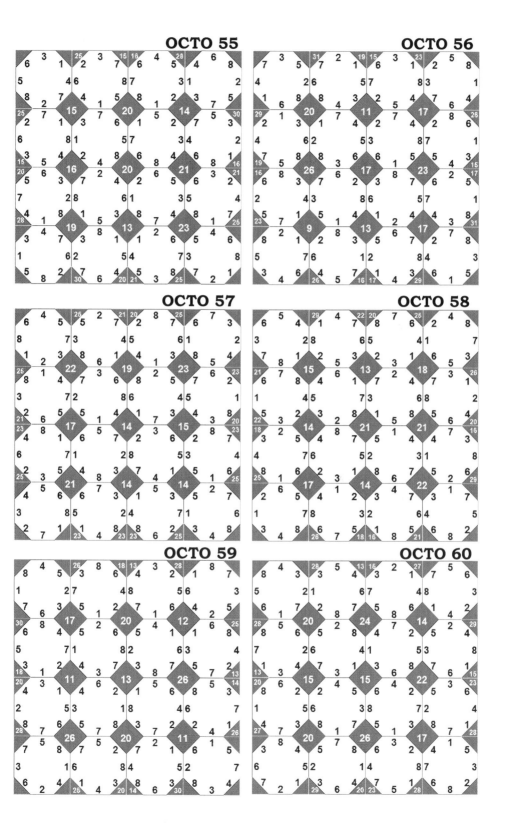

Made in the USA
Charleston, SC
26 November 2013